USING THIS BOOK

*Children learn to read by **reading**, but they need help to begin with.*

When you have read the story on the left-hand pages aloud to the child, go back to the beginning of the book and look at the pictures together.

Encourage children to read the sentences under the pictures. If they don't know a word, give them a chance to 'guess' what it is from the illustrations, before telling them.

There are more suggestions for helping children to learn to read in the *Parent/Teacher* booklet.

---

*Note: In this story the Griffle helps the children to escape from a thief. But the Griffle may not **always** be there when they need help.*

An opportunity to explain to children the possible dangers of talking to strangers occurs in this story.

British Library Cataloguing in Publication Data
McCullagh, Sheila K.
  The Griffle and the thief. — (Puddle Lane
  reading programme. Stage 2; v. 11)
  I. Title   II. Aitchison, Martin   III. Series
  823.914[J]   PZ7
  ISBN 0-7214-0927-X

First edition

Published by Ladybird Books Ltd Loughborough Leicestershire UK
Ladybird Books Inc Lewiston Maine 04240 USA

The Griffle
and the thief

written by SHEILA McCULLAGH
illustrated by MARTIN AITCHISON

This book belongs to:

Ladybird Books

One day, just before Christmas,
Sarah and Davy went down Puddle Lane.

Sarah and Davy
went down Puddle Lane.

5

Sarah and Davy were going to see
their grandmother.
Grandmother lived in Bread Street.
She had a white house, with a green door.

Sarah and Davy
went to see Grandmother.
Grandmother lived in a
white house with a green door.

Grandmother was very glad
to see them.
She gave them each a little cake, and
then they sat down to play games.
Then Grandmother read a story.
And then it was time
to have dinner.

Grandmother gave Sarah
and Davy a little cake.

After dinner, it was time to go home.
Grandmother went to the cupboard.
She took out two baskets.

Grandmother went
to the cupboard.
She took out two baskets.

"It's time to go home,"
said Grandmother.
"Take these baskets home with you.
There are Christmas presents
for you all. One of the presents
is for your mother.
It is a beautiful golden brooch.
My mother gave it to me,
when I was a girl.
So you must be very careful
with the baskets.
Go straight home.
Don't stop on the way."

Grandmother said,
"It's time to go home.
Take the baskets
home with you.
Don't stop on the way."

Sarah and Davy each took
one of the baskets.
They said "Goodbye" to Grandmother,
and started for home.

Sarah and Davy
took the baskets.

But as they went along,
they came to a shop.
The shop window was full
of things for Christmas.
There were plum puddings and
Christmas cakes.
There were boxes of sweets.
There were nuts and dates
and piles of fruit.
Sarah and Davy stopped to look
in the shop window,
and they stayed there
for a very long time.
At last, Sarah said,
"We must go home.
Grandmother said,
'Don't stop on the way.'"

Sarah and Davy
saw a shop window.
They stopped to look
in the window.
Sarah said,
''It's time to go home.
Grandmother said,
'Don't stop on the way.' ''

They hadn't gone far,
when they came to a toy shop.
The shop window was full
of things for Christmas.
There were castles and soldiers.
There were all kinds of games.
There were dolls and bears and monsters.
(One of the monsters looked a bit
like the Griffle.)
Sarah and Davy stopped
to look in the shop window.
They stayed for a very long time.
At last, Davy said,
"It's time to go home.
Grandmother said,
'Don't stop on the way.'"

Sarah and Davy saw a toy shop.
They stopped to look
in the window.
Davy said, "It's time to go home.
Grandmother said,
'Don't stop on the way.'"

As they came to the square,
they saw a big Christmas tree
with coloured balls and lanterns
hanging from the branches.
"It must have been put up
while we were having dinner,"
said Sarah.
The lanterns were all lit,
and they shone red and blue
and green and yellow.
Sarah and Davy stopped
to look at the tree,
and they stayed for
a very long time.
At last, Sarah said,
"It's time to go home.
Grandmother said,
'Don't stop on the way.'
And we have stopped three times!"

Sarah and Davy saw a tree.
They stopped to look
at the tree.
Sarah said,
''It's time to go home.
Grandmother said,
'Don't stop on the way.' And
we have stopped three times!''

They ran across the square,
and down the street
which led to Puddle Lane.
The sun was beginning to set.
They hurried along, because
they knew that they were late.
They didn't see two green ears,
up in the air, at the corner
of the lane.

Sarah and Davy ran.
They came to Puddle Lane.
They didn't see two green ears.

As they turned the corner
into Puddle Lane,
they saw a big man standing there.
They had never seen him before.
He looked very fierce.
"What have you got there?"
he demanded. "What have you got
in those baskets?"
Sarah and Davy stopped.

"Give me the baskets!"
said the man.

"We won't!" said Sarah.
She took a step back.

They saw a big man
in Puddle Lane.
The man said,
"Give me the baskets!"
"We won't!" said Sarah.

"You can't have our baskets,"
she said. "They belong to Grandmother.
And they belong to us."

"Give me the baskets!"
said the big man. "Hand them over!"

"We won't!" said Davy.
"You're a thief!"

The big man said,
"Give me the baskets!"
"We won't!" said Davy.

"If you won't give them to me,
I'll take them!" said the man.
And he stepped forward
to take the baskets.
But as he reached out
to seize the baskets,
Sarah saw a long green tail.
"It's the Griffle!" said Sarah.
"The Griffle is here.
The Griffle will help us."

Sarah saw a long green tail.
"It's the Griffle!" said Sarah.
"The Griffle is here.
The Griffle will help us."

The tail jerked – and the big man
fell over. He fell flat on his face!
As he got up again, he saw the Griffle!
The green Griffle was standing
there by the children.
"Oh, Griffle," said Davy,
"I'm **so** glad to see you!"

The big man fell over.
As he got up again,
he saw the Griffle!
"Oh, Griffle," said Davy.
"I'm so glad to see you."

The big man didn't stop
to talk to the Griffle.
He let out a loud yell, and fled.
He ran away as fast as he could.
He ran faster than he had ever run
in his life before.
He ran so fast, he fell over again.
But he got up, and ran on.

The big man ran away.
He ran so fast,
he fell over again.
But he got up,
and ran on.

The Griffle turned to the children.
"**He** won't come back to Puddle Lane again,"
he said.

"Oh, thank you, Griffle,"
said Sarah.

"I'm so glad you were there!"
said Davy.

"**He** won't come back
to Puddle Lane again,"
said the Griffle.

"I'm so glad you were there!"
said Davy.

The Griffle went back up Puddle Lane
with Sarah and Davy.
He waited until they had opened
the door of their house.
Then he vanished.

The Griffle went back
up Puddle Lane,
with Sarah and Davy.

Sarah and Davy had a wonderful Christmas.
Grandmother had sent
all kinds of presents.
(She must have been to the toy shop.)
And she had made a big Christmas cake
for them.
Sarah cut a large slice of Christmas cake
for the Griffle.
She went up to the end of the lane
with Davy, and they put the cake
on the garden wall.
They didn't see the Griffle
take the cake.
But when they went back an hour later,
the cake had gone.

Sarah and Davy put the cake
on the garden wall,
for the Griffle.

I Spy is a useful reading game.
Use this picture to play it.
"I spy with my little eye
something beginning with..."
*(Give the **sound** of the first
letter of the word to be
guessed, not the name.)*

Notes for the parent/teacher

When you have read the story, go back to the beginning. Look at each picture and talk about it, pointing to the caption below, and reading it aloud yourself.

Run your finger along under the words as you read, so that the child learns that reading goes from left to right. (You needn't say this in so many words. Children learn many useful things about reading by just reading with you, and it is often better to let them learn by experience, rather than by explanation.) When you next go through the book, encourage the child to read the words and sentences under the illustrations.

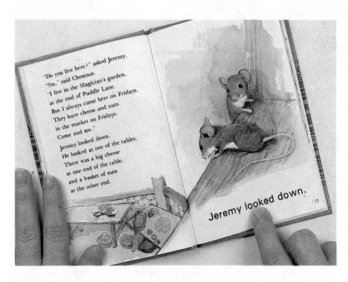

Jeremy looked down.

Don't rush in with the word before she* has time to think, but don't leave her struggling for too long. Always encourage her to feel that she is reading successfully, praising her when she does well, and avoiding criticism.

Now turn back to the beginning, and print the child's name in the space on the title page, using ordinary, not capital letters. Let her watch you print it: this is another useful experience.

*Children enjoy hearing the same story many times. Read this one as often as the child likes hearing it. The more opportunities she has of looking at the illustrations and **reading** the captions with you, the more she will come to recognise the words. Don't worry if she **remembers** rather than **reads** the captions. This is a normal stage in learning.*

If you have a number of books, let her choose which story she would like to have again.

**Footnote:* In order to avoid the continual "he or she", "him or her", the child is referred to in this book as "she". However, the stories are equally appropriate to boys and girls.

*Have you read these stories at **Stage 2** about the monsters and people who live in Puddle Lane?*

Stage 2

3 The little
  monster
5 The Gruffle
6 The Tidy Bird

*from The
little monster*

from The Tidy Bird